UNBREAKABLE

THE ART OF MOVING FORWARD

MONICA

Made with ♥ on the Notion Press Platform
www.notionpress.com

"I dedicate this book to my husband, Vaibhav Singh, whose unwavering support and companionship have been my anchor during life's most challenging times. Your love has redefined partnership and marriage for me, and I am eternally grateful.

And to my first and only child, Tzar, my beloved dog, whose unconditional love and loyalty have brought immense joy and comfort to my life."

Contents

Preface

In a world that often equates comfort with success, it's easy to find ourselves settling into routines that, while familiar, may not truly fulfill us. This book emerges from a personal journey—a journey marked by moments of profound discomfort, introspection, and ultimately, transformation.

Throughout my life, I've encountered challenges that forced me to question my beliefs, confront my fears, and step beyond the confines of my comfort zone. These experiences have taught me that true growth doesn't stem from ease but from embracing the unknown and pushing our boundaries.

This book is a culmination of those lessons. It's a guide for anyone seeking to break free from mediocrity, to harness the power of their subconscious, and to navigate the complexities of human relationships and personal growth. Each chapter delves into themes that have been pivotal in my own evolution, offering insights and strategies to help you on your path.

I invite you to embark on this journey with an open mind and a courageous heart. Together, let's explore the art of becoming unbreakable.

PROLOGUE

In the quiet moments of our lives, when the noise of the world fades, we often find ourselves reflecting on the paths we've taken. We ponder the dreams that once ignited our spirits, the challenges that tested our resolve, and the growth that emerged from our struggles.

This book is a journey into the depths of personal transformation. It's about understanding that comfort can be a silent adversary, lulling us into complacency and hindering our potential. It's about recognizing that our early experiences shape our desires, but it's our conscious choices that define our destiny.

Through these chapters, we'll explore the cycles of success and decline, the power of pain as a catalyst for growth, and the strength found in selective detachment. We'll delve into the essence of being present, the art of giving our all without regret, and the unyielding pursuit of self-respect.

This is not just a collection of thoughts but a call to action—a reminder that becoming unbreakable is a continuous journey, one that requires introspection, resilience, and an unwavering commitment to oneself.

As you embark on this journey, may you find the courage to face discomfort, the wisdom to learn from your past, and the strength to carve out the life you truly desire.

Chapter 4: Moving On Without Forgiving or Forgetting

Why you don't have to forgive to heal

Letting go vs. holding on to negativity

Becoming indifferent as a form of strength

Chapter 5: Facing the Pain Without Letting It Consume You

Accepting that pain never really leaves

How to deal with difficult moments without spiraling

Taking emotions as they come, then moving forward

Chapter 6: Cutting Out the Wrong People Without Guilt

The importance of choosing who you invest in

Why cutting people off isn't selfish, it's necessary

Learning to detach and protect your peace

Chapter 7: Giving 100%, Then Walking Away Without Regret

Why effort matters more than the outcome

Knowing when to move on

The freedom of being all in, then letting go

Chapter 8: The Art of Being Present & Unshakable

How to stay grounded in the present

Letting go of overthinking & unnecessary emotional weight

Thriving instead of just surviving

Chapter 9: Why Most People Settle for Less

The Comfort Trap

If You've Never Seen More, You Won't Crave More

The Cost of Staying Small

How to Break the Cycle

You Have Nothing to Lose—But Everything to Gain

I

Introduction

There comes a point in life when you realize that nothing changes until you decide to change. People often talk about transformation like it's some grand revelation, a lightning bolt moment where everything suddenly falls into place. But the truth is, growth isn't about waiting for inspiration to strike—it's about making a choice, again and again, every single day.

I've always believed that life is shaped by our mindset. It's not about what happens to us, but how we choose to respond. Some people hit rock bottom and stay there, blaming circumstances, people, or bad luck. Others use it as a stepping stone, a launching pad for something greater. The difference between these two kinds of people isn't intelligence, talent, or privilege—it's the way they think.

I won't tell you that the journey is easy. It never gets easier. In fact, it often gets harder. But I've come to accept that, and I've learned that real strength doesn't come from avoiding pain or forgetting the past. It comes from using it. From remembering why you started in the first place, from refusing to fall back into the same traps, from being so unshakable in your commitment to yourself that nothing can pull you back into mediocrity.

This book isn't about empty motivation. It's about reality—the struggles, the setbacks, the moments when everything feels unbearable. It's about understanding that pain doesn't disappear, but it can fuel you. It's about learning to give your 100% to something and, when it no longer serves you, moving on without regret. It's about not wasting your energy on things or people that drain you.

Most importantly, it's about choosing yourself. Because if there's one thing I know for sure, it's that no one is coming to save you. You have to make the choice.

This is not a guide to an easy life. This is a guide to an unbreakable mindset.

The Shift That Changed Everything

There was a time when I found myself trapped in cycles—cycles of pain, disappointment, and expectations that never seemed to align with reality. I used to wonder why things never got better, why no matter how much effort I put in, certain people and situations always brought the same negativity.

Then one day, I stopped wondering and started deciding. I decided to change—not in a superficial way, but in a way that redefined how I saw the world and, more importantly, how I saw myself.

This book isn't just about resilience. It's not about telling you to "think positive" or "move on" in a way that disregards reality. It's about a mindset shift—a perspective that transforms struggles into fuel, detachment into power, and presence into a way of life.

I want you to read this book as if we are having a conversation—because every word comes from my own experiences, reflections, and realizations. I won't sugarcoat things, and I won't tell you that life will suddenly become easy. But I will tell you that you can train your mind to be unbreakable, to stop falling back into the same emotional traps, and to keep moving forward—no matter what.

II

The Power of Mindset

There was a time when I believed that life was just unfair—things didn't get better, struggles never really ended, and people rarely changed. And to an extent, I was right. Life doesn't get better on its own. Struggles do keep coming. And most people don't change.

But then I realized something.

It wasn't life that needed to change. It was me.

Why Mindset is Everything

The most powerful realization I ever had was your mindset dictates everything. It's not about what happens to you—it's about how you process it, how you react, and what you do next.

I used to spend so much time wondering why people acted the way they did, why things didn't go the way I expected, and why I always felt let down. But then I stopped asking those questions and started asking new ones:

What do I want?
What am I willing to tolerate?
What am I willing to do to move forward?

That shift changed everything.

Because here's the truth—struggles are inevitable. But suffering? That's a choice.

The Difference Between Those Who Stay Stuck and Those Who Rise

I've seen two kinds of people in life.

The first kind are the ones who stay stuck. They keep complaining about the same things, keep blaming circumstances, keep waiting for something external to change before they take action. These people let life happen to them.

Then there are the ones who rise. These people don't waste time complaining. They don't wait for the "right time" or for circumstances to magically improve. They take control, no matter how hard it gets. They keep moving forward, no matter what.

The difference? Mindset.

It's not about having an easier life or avoiding struggles. It's about how you face them.

Do you let them break you?
Or do you use them as fuel?

I chose the second path.

Understanding That Struggle is a Choice

I used to think pain was something I had no control over. That, when something hurt me, I had to dwell on it, process it endlessly, and let it affect my energy.

Now, I don't let pain linger longer than necessary.

I give myself 10 minutes to feel bad when something goes wrong. That's it. 10 minutes. After that, I shift my focus back to what matters. I don't sit in the negativity. I don't replay the hurt over and over. I don't let it define me.

Struggle, in its purest form, is a choice. Yes, things will go wrong. Yes, people will disappoint you. Yes, life will be unfair. But whether you let that consume you or push you forward? That part is entirely up to you.

And that's where power lies.

The Mindset Shift That Changes Everything

The day I stopped expecting life to be easy was the day I became unstoppable. I no longer asked, "Why is this happening to me?" Instead, I started asking, "How do I make the most of this?"

That's the shift.

That's the difference between being stuck and rising above.

The truth is, life doesn't get better. You get better.

And once you understand that, nothing can break you.

III
Comfort is the Enemy

There's a pattern I've seen play out time and time again—in my life, in the lives of others, and in every success story that turned into stagnation. It goes like this:

Struggle – You fight, you push, you hustle. You work through the pain because you have no other choice.

Success – You achieve something, whether big or small. You reach a milestone. The hard work starts paying off.

Comfort – You relax. You stop pushing as hard. You start believing you don't need to fight anymore.

Decline – You lose the edge, the hunger, the fire. And before you realize it, you're back at square one, wondering what went wrong.

This cycle is the reason why people fail, even after they succeed.

Why Do People Fall Back After Achieving Something?

I've always believed that people don't just stop growing. They choose comfort over growth, even if they don't realize it.

It happens when people forget the pain that pushed them in the first place. They forget what it felt like to struggle, to fight, to want something so badly that they were willing to endure anything to get it. And once they reach a certain level, they think they can afford to relax.

But the moment you relax, the moment you believe you've made it, that's when the decline begins.

I've seen it happen in relationships, careers, personal growth—everywhere. Someone fights to escape a bad situation, but once they're out, they stop working on themselves. They stop improving. And eventually, they end up right where they started, making the same mistakes all over again.

They go back to toxic people.
They let their ambitions fade.

Bottomline, they become comfortable.

And comfort is the enemy.

Staying Uncomfortable to Keep Growing

I don't allow myself to get comfortable.

That doesn't mean I don't enjoy my successes or appreciate how far I've come. It means I never let myself believe the work is over. Because the moment you think you've arrived, you stop moving forward.

I remind myself of the struggles, not to dwell on them, but to fuel me. I don't let myself forget what it took to get here, so I don't make the mistake of slipping back into the mindset that trapped me before.

Growth only happens in discomfort.

That's why the most successful people keep pushing, even when they don't have to. The moment they reach one goal, they set another. They don't allow comfort to dull their drive.

If you want to keep growing, you have to make discomfort your new normal. You have to be okay with feeling stretched, challenged, and uncertain. You have to choose to stay hungry, no matter how much you achieve.

Because the second you get too comfortable, you stop moving forward. And that's when everything starts to fall apart.

Comfort is the enemy. Stay uncomfortable, and you'll never

stop rising.

IV

Remember What Started the Fire

People say time heals all wounds, but I disagree. Time distances you from pain, but it doesn't erase it. And in some ways, that distance is dangerous. Because the more time passes, the more we forget what the struggle felt like.

We forget the nights we cried ourselves to sleep.
We forget the frustration of being stuck.
We forget the fire that made us fight for more.

And the moment we forget, we risk falling right back into the same mistakes that once broke us.

Why You Shouldn't Forget Your Struggles

I've seen this happen with people who escape toxic relationships, only to go back. At first, they knew why they left. They remembered the hurt, the betrayal, the exhaustion of trying to fix something that was never meant to be fixed. But time softens the edges of those memories. They start to think, Maybe it wasn't that bad. They romanticize the past, ignoring the reality of what it really was.

And just like that, they're back in the same situation, learning the same painful lesson all over again.

It's not just about relationships. It happens in careers, in personal growth, in every part of life. People work hard to get somewhere, but once they do, they let go of the mindset that got them there in the first place. They stop pushing. They stop remembering why they had to fight so hard.

And before they know it, they've lost everything they built.

Using Pain as Fuel, Not as an Anchor

I don't believe in dwelling on the past. Holding onto pain in a way that weighs you down only traps you in bitterness and regret. But there's a difference between carrying your pain as a burden and using it as fuel.

I keep my struggles close, not to suffer from them, but to stay sharp. I remind myself of what I went through, so I don't become complacent. I use that memory to keep moving forward, not to look back.

The key is to strike a balance—remember your pain, but don't let it control you. Let it be a reminder, not a chain.

Pain isn't meant to keep you stuck. It's meant to push you forward.

Avoiding the Trap of Repeating Past Mistakes

The biggest mistake people make is thinking they've learned their lesson, only to repeat the same cycle again. That's what happens when you forget why you had to fight so hard in the first place.

If you don't consciously remember, life will force you to remember—by putting you through the same suffering again. And again. Until you finally get it.

That's why I make sure I never forget.

I don't need to dwell in pain, but I refuse to erase it from my memory. That pain shaped me. That struggle built me. And if I ever let myself forget, I know I'll risk slipping back into things I worked so hard to escape.

So, I choose to remember.

I remember what started the fire inside me.
I remember what I've been through.
And I make sure I never let myself go through it again.

V

Moving On Without Forgiving or Forgetting

People talk a lot about forgiveness like it's the ultimate solution to healing. "Just forgive and let go," they say, as if it's that easy. As if every betrayal, every hurt, every disappointment can just be wiped away with a simple act of forgiveness.

But here's the truth—not everyone or everything deserves forgiveness. And that's okay.

Why You Don't Have to Forgive to Heal

There's a common belief that forgiveness is necessary for closure. That unless you forgive, you'll stay trapped in anger or resentment. But I don't agree. Forgiveness isn't the only path to healing. In fact, sometimes, it's not even the right one.

Why should I forgive someone who knowingly hurt me? Why should I excuse actions that broke me?

Some people don't deserve that kind of release. And I'm not God. It's not my job to grant everyone peace at the cost of my own.

What I choose instead is indifference. I don't need to forgive, but I also don't need to carry the weight of what happened. I don't sit with anger or bitterness—I just move on. The past is the past, and I refuse to let it have power over me anymore.

Letting Go vs. Holding On to Negativity

Some people think not forgiving means you're stuck in the past, that you're holding on to negativity. But it's actually the opposite. Holding on is when you keep replaying the situation in your head, reliving the pain over and over.

Letting go is when you stop giving it energy.

I don't forgive, but I also don't dwell. I acknowledge what happened, I accept that it was unfair, and then I move forward. I don't waste my time seeking revenge, or waiting for apologies that will never come. I focus on myself, my growth, my future.

And that's how I win.

Becoming Indifferent as a Form of Strength

The strongest thing you can do is become indifferent.

Not bitter.
Not angry.
Not obsessed with making things right.

Just indifferent.

Because the opposite of love isn't hate—it's indifference. Hate still means you care. It still means they have a hold over you. But when you become indifferent, when they no longer affect your thoughts, your emotions, your life—that's when you're truly free.

I don't need to forgive, and I definitely won't forget. What happened shaped me, and I take those lessons with me. But I refuse to let the past keep me stuck.

I move on, not because I forgive, but because I refuse to let it define me.

And that's all the closure I need.

VI

Facing the Pain Without Letting It Consume You

Pain is not something you can just erase. It doesn't magically disappear with time, nor does it fade completely, no matter how much you heal. It stays—sometimes quietly in the background, sometimes hitting you out of nowhere. And that's the thing about pain: it never really leaves.

But just because it stays doesn't mean it has to consume you.

I've learned that the key is facing it, not fearing it. You don't have to pretend you're unaffected. You don't have to shove it down and act like everything is fine. Instead, you acknowledge it, feel it, but you don't let it break you.

Accepting That Pain Never Really Leaves

People say, "It'll get better with time." But does it? Does it ever truly get better?

I don't think so. It just gets... different. You learn how to carry it better, how to keep moving despite it. But some wounds never fully close, and that's okay.

The problem isn't that the pain exists—it's what you do with it. Some people let it define them, let it shape their entire existence. But I refuse to live like that. Pain is a part of me, but it is not all of me.

There are moments when it resurfaces, when it tries to pull me back down. And in those moments, I remind myself: I have been through worse, and I have survived every single time.

How to Deal With Difficult Moments Without Spiraling

Difficult moments come unexpectedly. They creep in when you least expect it—when you're alone, when you're already tired, when something triggers an old memory. And suddenly, you're back in that dark place.

So how do you stop yourself from spiraling?

I take it as it comes. I don't overthink it. I don't try to fight it. The more you resist, the harder it grips you. Instead, I let it pass through me.

I give myself permission to feel. If I need ten minutes to sit with my emotions, I take them. I let myself feel sad, angry, disappointed—but I do not stay there. I remind myself that this moment will pass, just like it always has.

Because if you let yourself drown in every painful moment, you'll never move forward. You are allowed to feel—but you are not allowed to be consumed.

Taking Emotions as They Come, Then Moving Forward

There's a difference between acknowledging pain and living in it.

I allow myself moments of weakness, but I don't allow them to define my day, my week, my life. If I feel low for ten minutes, so be it. I accept it. But after those ten minutes? I get back up.

I don't dwell.
I don't overanalyze.
I move on.

That's the mindset that keeps me strong—not by ignoring pain, but by refusing to let it have power over me.

Because at the end of the day, pain will always be there in some form. But I get to decide whether I carry it as a burden or use it as fuel.

And I choose to move forward. Always.

VII

Cutting Out the Wrong People Without Guilt

One of the most liberating things I've learned is that you don't owe anyone a place in your life. Not everyone deserves access to you.

There was a time when I believed in giving endless chances, in holding onto people simply because of history or obligation. But the truth is, people show you who they are. And when they show you that they don't respect you, don't value you, or don't reciprocate your effort, you need to believe them and act accordingly.

Cutting people off isn't about being cold or heartless—it's about protecting your peace. And if that makes me selfish in someone's eyes, so be it.

The Importance of Choosing Who You Invest In

Energy is limited. Time is limited. And who you give those things to shapes your life more than you realize.

I've learned to be careful about who I invest in. If I am giving someone my time, my support, my energy, I expect it to mean something. But when you continuously give and receive nothing in return—whether it's respect, appreciation, or basic decency—it's time to rethink that investment.

Some people take it without giving. They drain you. They disrespect your boundaries. They don't value what you bring to the table. Why should you keep them in your life?

If someone repeatedly shows you that they don't deserve your presence, let them go. Not with anger. Not with hatred. Just with clarity.

Why Cutting People Off Isn't Selfish, It's Necessary

People think cutting someone off is cruel. But staying in situations that drain you is crueler—to yourself.

I used to feel guilty about walking away. I would overthink it, wondering if I was being too harsh. But I realized something: every time I kept the wrong people around, I was betraying myself.

You are not responsible for carrying dead weight. You are not required to endure mistreatment just because you once cared about someone. Relationships—whether friendships, family, or anything else—should be built on mutual respect and effort.

If it's one-sided, if it's toxic, if it's draining—cut it out. No explanations are needed. No guilt is required.

Learning to Detach and Protect Your Peace

The hardest part is detaching.

Sometimes, we hold on because of history. "They were there for me once." Or we justify things: "Maybe they'll change." But holding onto the wrong people doesn't change them—it just prevents you from growing.

Detachment is a skill. It takes practice. But once you master it, you'll see how freeing it is.

I no longer allow myself to be emotionally entangled with people who don't value me. If someone isn't treating me right, if they are bringing negativity into my life, I distance myself—mentally, emotionally, and physically.

Because at the end of the day, your peace is your responsibility. And if someone threatens that peace, you don't argue, you don't beg, you don't explain.

You simply walk away.

VIII

Giving 100%, Then Walking Away Without Regret

One of the most powerful mindsets I've adopted is to give everything your best, and then walk away without regret.

There was a time when I used to overthink, wondering if I could have done something differently, if I should have held on a little longer, or if I had made a mistake by letting go. But now, I live by one simple rule: if I gave my 100%, then there's nothing left to question.

Why Effort Matters More Than the Outcome

We can't control outcomes. We can't control how people react, how situations unfold, or whether something works out in our favour. But what we can control is how much we put in.

That's why I believe in going all in. Whether it's work, relationships, or personal growth—if I commit to something, I give it everything I have.

Because if I don't, then I'll always wonder what if?

But when I know I gave my best, when I know I showed up fully and did everything I could, then I can move on without looking back. There is nothing worse than regret over things you didn't try hard enough for.

Knowing When to Move On

There is a fine line between persistence and wasting time.

Some people stay in situations far longer than they should, not because they're still trying but because they're afraid of letting go. They keep waiting for things to change, for people to act differently, for circumstances to align. But waiting is not the same as progress.

I've learned to recognize when something has run its course. When I've given all I could and it's still not working, I don't beg, I don't force—I walk away.

And here's the truth: moving on is not failure. Staying in a place that no longer serves you is.

The Freedom of Being All In, Then Letting Go

There is an incredible sense of peace in knowing you did everything you could.

When you live like this, there is no resentment, no grudges, no regrets—just clarity. You don't have to carry the weight of "what ifs" because you already did what needed to be done.

I've applied this to every area of my life. In work, I give my best effort. If it succeeds, great. If it doesn't, I move on. In relationships, I put in genuine effort. If it's reciprocated, it grows. If it's not, I let go.

No guilt. No second-guessing.

Because at the end of the day, if you've given your 100%, you owe nothing more.

IX

The Art of Being Present & Unshakable

Life is not meant to be spent in endless loops of overthinking, regret, or fear of the future. Yet, that's exactly where most people get stuck—either obsessing over what happened or stressing over what's to come. But I've realized something: the only way to truly live is to be present.

Not just physically, but mentally, emotionally, and fully.

How to Stay Grounded in the Present

Being present is not just about "living in the moment" in some cliché way. It's about fully engaging with whatever you are doing, whoever you are with, and wherever you are without distractions from the past or the future.

I've trained myself to focus on what's in front of me, rather than wasting time reliving old pain or worrying about things I cannot control.

If I'm working, I am fully working.

If I'm resting, I allow myself to rest without guilt.

If I'm spending time with someone, I give them my full attention.

It's a discipline—one that has helped me break free from the mental chaos that comes with constantly overanalyzing life.

Letting Go of Overthinking & Unnecessary Emotional Weight

I used to carry too much. Every past hurt, every bad experience, every wrong word spoken by someone—I let it sit in my mind like a heavy weight.

But I realized something: carrying pain doesn't make you stronger. Letting go does.

That doesn't mean forgetting or pretending things didn't happen. It means not giving those things the power to drain you anymore.

Overthinking doesn't change anything. It doesn't fix the past or guarantee a better future. All it does is steal your energy from the present.

So, I stopped giving my time and energy to thoughts that only pulled me backwards. Instead, I take things as they come. I don't sit and plan how to deal with pain or difficult moments—I face them when they arrive and move on. I don't let them take over my mind before they even happen.

Thriving Instead of Just Surviving

Most people are just surviving—dragging themselves through life, dealing with one thing after another, never really feeling alive. But I refuse to live like that.

For me, thriving means owning my time, my energy, and my emotions. It means making peace with my past, not worrying too much about the future, and focusing on what I can do right now.

Even if I have 10 minutes in a day where I feel low, I let myself feel it. But I don't let it take over. I get back up. Because life is too short to be stuck in negativity.

Being present is the key to being unshakable. When you're here, now, fully in the moment—nothing from the past can haunt you, and nothing from the future can scare you. You just exist, grow, and move forward.

And that, to me, is real strength.

X

Why Most People Settle for Less

Most people don't settle for mediocrity because they have to. They settle because it's easier.

They convince themselves that what they have is "good enough." They tell themselves they don't need more, that they're fine where they are. Not because they truly believe it, but because aiming higher would mean stepping into the unknown.

And stepping into the unknown? That's uncomfortable.

It means effort. It means taking risks. It means leaving behind the familiar and working for something they might not get right away. And most people would rather stay where they are than face that kind of uncertainty.

The Comfort Trap

Once you start settling, you stop dreaming.

You tell yourself, "I don't need a better job. This one pays the bills."
You tell yourself, "I don't need to push harder. At least I'm doing okay."
You tell yourself, "I don't need that big goal. What I have is enough."

And the worst part? You start believing it.

At first, you might feel a little regret, a little longing for more. But over time, you silence that voice. You convince yourself that aiming higher is unnecessary. You shrink your ambitions. You settle into a routine.

And before you know it, years pass, and you wonder why you never pushed yourself.

If You've Never Seen More, You Won't Crave More

The reason most people settle is because they've never experienced anything greater. They don't even know what's possible.

Think about it: If someone has only ever traveled 50 kilometers from their hometown, they'll think that's the extent of adventure. If they've only ever earned just enough to survive, they won't believe financial freedom is realistic.

They've never tasted the next level.

And if you've never tasted it, you don't crave it.

That's why breaking out of mediocrity isn't just about motivation—it's about exposure.

The Cost of Staying Small

Settling for less isn't just about missing opportunities—it's about missing yourself.

You never get to see what you're capable of. You never push your limits. You never know what you could have achieved if you had just tried harder, just taken that risk, just refused to settle.

You may think you're choosing comfort, but in reality, you're choosing regret.

Because one day, you'll look back and wonder:

"What if I had pushed a little harder?"
"What if I had taken that leap?"
"What if I had refused to settle?"

And by then, it's too late.

How to Break the Cycle

If you don't want to end up like everyone else—stuck, comfortable, and looking back with regret—you have to break the cycle now.

Stop justifying mediocrity. If you catch yourself thinking, "This is fine," ask yourself: Is it really? Or are you just avoiding the work required to have something better?

Expose yourself to more. If you've never seen success, find people who have it. If you've never traveled, read about those who have. Expand your vision.

Embrace discomfort. Growth is painful. The sooner you accept that, the easier it becomes. The more you chase comfort, the more you block your own potential.

Stay desperate. Never let yourself get too comfortable. The moment you think you've "made it," find a new goal to chase.

You Have Nothing to Lose—But Everything to Gain

Right now, you might feel like you have something to lose by pushing for more. The risk, the uncertainty, the effort—it all seems like too much.

But the truth is, the real risk is staying the same.

Because the cost of mediocrity isn't just a smaller life—it's a life unlived.

XI

The Inner Calling—Why Some People Never See the Bigger Picture

You can show people a bigger picture, you can hand them the roadmap, you can tell them exactly what to do—but they won't get it.

They won't understand.

Not because they lack intelligence, but because they lack urgency.

Instead of being inspired, most people react with jealousy,

anger, or resentment. Not because you've done something wrong, but because deep down, they know they're not willing to do what it takes. That realization makes them uncomfortable. And that discomfort? It turns into negativity.

They don't want to leave their comfort zone, but they hate seeing someone else break free from it.

This is why trying to "wake people up" is pointless. People will only change when they are desperate.

Comfort Kills the Inner Calling

The biggest lie people tell themselves is, "One day, I'll do it."

They talk about their dreams, their goals, the life they want. But they take no action. Because there is no urgency.

The truth is, as long as life is comfortable—even if it's mediocre—most people will stay exactly where they are.

No real calling comes in comfort.

It only comes when life pushes you to the edge, when you're forced to look at yourself and ask:

Am I okay with this being my life forever?

Is this all I'm capable of?

What happens if I don't change?

And when the answer to those questions is unbearable—that's when transformation starts.

Why Rock Bottom is a Gift

People who have never truly struggled will never understand the fire that comes from desperation.

When you hit your lowest point, you're given two choices:

Stay there. Let life break you. Accept mediocrity. Keep making excuses.

Fight like hell to rise. And never let yourself fall to that level again.

That's the moment when the inner calling happens.

You realize you have two options: change or stay stuck. And when staying stuck becomes more painful than the effort it takes to change, you will do whatever it takes.

This is why some people never unlock their full potential. Because their life has never forced them to.

They have never experienced the kind of pain that forces self-reflection. They have never faced the kind of struggle that makes them desperate for change.

And because of that, they will stay where they are—forever waiting for "the right time."

The Challenge: Staying Hungry After Breaking Free

The real problem isn't just breaking free. It's staying free.

Most people push themselves only until they escape pain. They work hard until they achieve some success, until they reach a place of stability.

Then?

They fall right back into comfort.

They start taking things for granted. They lose the hunger that got them there in the first place.

That's why very few people sustain greatness.

It's not just about breaking free once—it's about maintaining that hunger even when life gets good.

The ones who truly achieve something in life are the ones who never stop pushing, who never let themselves settle, who refuse to get comfortable.

They remember what started the fire. They never forget the struggle that made them who they are.

And because of that, they never stop growing.

XII

Unlocking the Subconscious Blueprint

Most people think of destiny as something external—some grand plan written in the stars, something beyond their control. But what if destiny isn't outside of us?

What if it's something we created long ago, deep in our subconscious?

A blueprint that's been shaping our lives all along, guiding our choices without us even realizing it?

Destiny Isn't Fate—It's a Reflection of the Mind

Destiny isn't some unchangeable force dictating our lives. It's simply the unfolding of our deepest beliefs, desires, and fears.

Think about it -- Have you ever had a moment where you just knew something was going to happen? A gut feeling that a certain path was meant for you? That wasn't magic—it was your subconscious revealing a plan you'd already built.

But here's the problem. Most people don't consciously shape their blueprint. They let their fears, doubts, and limitations write it for them. And when fear writes your destiny, you stay small. You stay stuck. You never reach the life you were meant for.

Why Most People Never Unlock Their Destiny

The reason most people never reach their true potential isn't because they lack talent, intelligence, or opportunity. It's because they never unlock the deeper layers of their subconscious where their true power lies.

They don't believe they can. If you've spent your whole life believing success is for "other people," your subconscious will keep proving you right.

They live in fear. Fear of failure, fear of rejection, fear of losing what they already have—these fears keep them from taking the necessary risks.

They don't sustain their power. Everyone has moments of clarity—times when they fight, when they push, when they break through. But once the moment passes, they slip back into comfort.

The Moments We Unlock Our Full Potential

Think back to the hardest moment in your life. A time when you felt trapped, desperate, with no way out.

What happened?

You found a way.

You became stronger. You pushed past limits you didn't even know existed. You unlocked something inside you.

That's the secret -- We all have this power. But most people only tap into it in survival mode. They use it when they have no other choice. The real challenge is staying in that state of clarity, drive, and belief even when things are comfortable.

Rewriting the Blueprint

If destiny is something we create in our subconscious, then we have the power to rewrite it.

Change the script in your mind. Stop saying, "I'll never be successful," and start saying, "I am capable of anything." Your subconscious listens.

Face your fears instead of avoiding them. Fear is what keeps your destiny locked away. The more you challenge it, the more control you gain.

Push yourself when you don't have to. Don't wait for a crisis to unlock your full potential. Train yourself to operate at that level every single day.

The Ones Who Unlock Their Destiny

Out of 100 people, maybe one will truly manifest their highest potential. Not because the others couldn't—but because they let fear, comfort, and hesitation keep them from trying.

The ones who create their own destiny aren't special. They're just the ones who refuse to settle. The ones who break through fear. The ones who learn to stay in that heightened state of belief and action, even when things get hard.

So the question is, "Are you going to be the one who unlocks it?" Or "are you going to let fear write your destiny for you?"

XIII

Conclusion: Becoming Unbreakable

Mindset is not something you switch on and off when life gets hard. It's a way of life. A commitment to yourself. A decision that, no matter what happens, you will not break. You will not allow circumstances, people, or emotions to shake your foundation.

Because at the end of the day, you are all you have.

Making This Mindset a Way of Life

Adopting this mindset isn't about being perfect. It's about being intentional. It's about knowing that life will throw challenges your way, but you are built to handle them.

You accept pain but don't let it consume you.

You remember your struggles but don't let them define you.

You invest in the right people and cut off the wrong ones—without guilt.

You give 100% to what matters, and if it still doesn't work, you walk away without regret.

You live in the present, not in past wounds or future anxieties.

This is how you make unbreakability a way of life. It's a practice, a discipline, and a promise to yourself that no matter what happens, you will rise.

Why Happiness Comes From Respecting Yourself

Most people search for happiness in external things—success, relationships, and approval from others. But true happiness is simpler than that. It comes from self-respect.

When you respect yourself, you stop tolerating things that drain you. You stop begging for love, validation, or fairness from people who don't deserve your energy. You don't lower your standards just to be accepted.

Respecting yourself means:

Knowing your worth, even when others don't.

Choosing peace over drama.

Letting go of anything that doesn't align with your growth.

Saying no without explaining yourself.

Walking away from what doesn't serve you, unapologetically.

Once you start living this way, happiness follows naturally. Not because life becomes perfect, but because you stop allowing unnecessary suffering into your life.

Choosing Yourself, Every Single Day

Every day, you wake up with a choice: To put yourself first or let the world dictate your life.

To be unbreakable, you must choose yourself. Every. Single. Day.

That doesn't mean being selfish—it means understanding that if you don't take care of yourself, no one else will. It means being your own protector, your own biggest supporter, and your own source of strength.

Because the truth is, no one is coming to save you.

No one will fight your battles for you.

No one will heal your wounds for you.

No one will create the life you want for you.

It's all on you.

And that's not a burden—that's power.

When you realize that everything you need is already within you, you become unstoppable. Nothing can break you because you don't rely on anything external to keep you whole.

This is what it means to be unbreakable.

Not being fearless, but facing fear head-on.
Not avoiding pain, but refusing to let it define you.
Not waiting for life to get easier, but becoming stronger than anything life throws at you.

And that, to me, is the ultimate freedom.

OTHER NOTABLE WORK

"Check out our other books - Unapologetic Words and Unapologetic Scribbles - Journey Of Broken Expectations."

9 7 9 8 8 9 7 4 4 0 6 0 3